Breakthrough Inventions

INVENTING THE TELEVISION

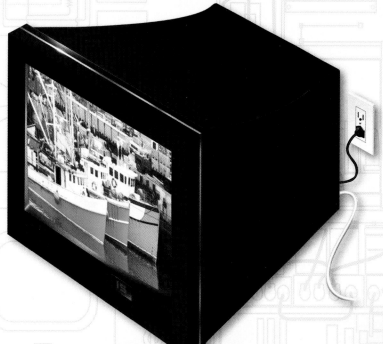

Joanne Richter

Crabtree Publishing Company

www.crabtreebooks.com

Breakthrough Inventions

Crabtree Publishing Company

www.crabtreebooks.com

Coordinating editor: Ellen Rodger

Series editor: Adrianna Morganelli

Project editor: L. Michelle Nielsen

Designer and production coordinator: Rosie Gowsell

Production assistant: Samara Parent

Scanning technician: Arlene Arch-Wilson

Art director: Rob MacGregor

Project development, editing, photo editing, and layout:
First Folio Resource Group, Inc.: Tom Dart, Greg Duhaney,
Sarah Gleadow, Debbie Smith

Photo research: Maria DeCambra, Melody Tolson

Consultants: Tom Genova, http://www.tvhistory.tv; Steve McVoy,
Early Television Foundation; John Trenouth, Head of Television at
the National Museum of Photography, Film & Television, UK

Photographs: AJ Photo/Hop Americain/Science Photo Library:
p. 29 (bottom); AP/World Wide Photo: p. 20, p. 24 (left), p. 30, p. 31
(top); Bettmann/Corbis: p. 13 (right), p. 15 (top), p. 16, p. 17 (left);
Corbis: p. 10 (right); CP/AP/Reed Saxon: p. 26 (top); CP/Everett
Collection: p. 19 (left); Jim Craigmyle/Corbis: p. 29 (top); George B.
Diebold/Corbis: p. 21 (left); Granger Collection, New York: p. 13
(left), p. 18 (right); E.O. Hoppé/Corbis: p. 5 (top); Hulton-Deutsch
Collection/Corbis: p. 8; Wolfgang Kaehler/Corbis: p. 4 (right);
Lake County Museum/Corbis: p. 14; Sean Locke/istock
International: cover (bottom right);

Mary Evans Picture Library: p. 24 (right); Hank Morgan/Photo
Researchers, Inc.: p. 31 (bottom); NASA/S69-39563: p. 26 (bottom);
NMPFT/Science & Society Picture Library: p. 9 (top); Oxford
Science Archive/Heritage-Images/The Image Works: p. 6 (left);
Greg Pease/Stone/Getty Images: p. 28 (top); Schenectady
Museum, Mike Segar/Reuters/Corbis: p. 25; Hall of Electrical;
Courtesy of Swann Auction Galleries: p. 6 (right); Reprinted and
copyrighted with permission of Tribunal Media Serves 2006: p. 18
(left); www.tvhistory.tv: p. 5 (bottom), p. 7, p. 9 (bottom), p. 10
(left), p. 11 (both), p. 15 (bottom), p. 17 (right); Warner Bros./Getty
Images: p. 19 (right); Worldspec/NASA/Alamy: p. 21 (right);
Other images from stock CD.

Illustrations: www.mikecarterstudio.com: title page, p. 3, p.12,
pp. 22–23

Cover: While inventing the television was not a simple task, it
proved to be an invention that changed the world. Over the years,
new technologies have improved the picture and sound quality of
televisions, and there are so many programs available that almost
everyone is sure to find a show they would love to watch.

Title page: Televisions have changed from sets that looked like
large pieces of furniture to smaller, but still bulky models. Some
of today's TVs are just flat screens hung on walls or from ceilings.

Contents page: Cathode-ray tubes (CRTs), found in many
television sets, are often recycled so that harmful materials inside,
such as a metal called lead, cannot enter the soil or water and
harm people and the environment.

Crabtree Publishing Company

www.crabtreebooks.com   1-800-387-7650

Cataloging-in-Publication Data
Richter, Joanne.
  Inventing the television / written by Joanne Richter.
        p. cm. -- (Breakthrough inventions)
  Includes bibliographical references and index.
  ISBN-13: 978-0-7787-2813-9 (rlb)
  ISBN-10: 0-7787-2813-7 (rlb)
  ISBN-13: 978-0-7787-2835-1 (pbk)
  ISBN-10: 0-7787-2835-8 (pbk)
1. Television--Juvenile literature. I. Title. II. Series.
  TK6640.R53 2006
  621.388--dc22
                                              2005035439
                                                  LC

**Published in
the United States**
PMB 16A
350 Fifth Ave.,
Suite 3308,
New York, NY
10118

**Published
in Canada**
616 Welland Ave.
St. Catharines,
Ontario, Canada
L2M 5V6

**Published in the
United Kingdom**
White Cross Mills
High Town, Lancaster,
LA1 4XS
United Kingdom

**Published
in Australia**
386 Mt. Alexander Rd.,
Ascot Vale (Melbourne)
VIC 3032

Contents

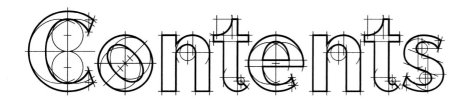

Before Television

M ore than one billion television sets around the world provide people with entertainment, education, and information. Television, or TV, is an invention that sends images and sound over distances and re-creates them on a screen and through speakers. "Tele" means "distant," so "television" means "distant vision," or "seeing over distance."

A Novel Idea

Before television was invented, people gathered around the radio to listen to news, comedy programs, dramatic series, and musical **variety shows**. They watched movies, musicals, and plays in theaters, and read newspapers, magazines, and books to keep informed and entertained.

Movie projectors, an invention that predates TV, show films by projecting, or displaying, images directly on a screen rather than sending them through cables or by satellite, *as televisions do.*

People can receive television programming almost anywhere by satellite, even in the desert.

Early Experiments in Communication

In the 1800s, inventors discovered new ways to communicate over distances. In 1837, the American inventor Samuel F. B. Morse used a machine called a telegraph to send written messages from one place to another. By tapping a switch on the telegraph, messages were translated into a code called Morse code, which was a series of electrical signals that were carried over wires.

The telephone became popular in the late 1870s, after developments made by Scottish-born inventor Alexander Graham Bell. Telephones allowed people to speak over distances by changing the sound of their voices into electrical signals.

The Wireless Radio

In 1895, Guglielmo Marconi, of Italy, transmitted, or sent, Morse code messages using a type of energy called radio waves. The radio waves carried messages through the air, from one **antenna** to another. Messages could travel over longer distances, and be sent and received by ships at sea.

(above) Marconi's wireless radio was the first invention that allowed a message to be broadcast, or sent, to many antennas at once.

The Birth of Broadcasting

On December 24, 1906, Canadian scientist Reginald A. Fessenden was the first to broadcast his voice, not just signals, over the radio. He shocked sailors on ships by reading from the Bible, wishing them, "Merry Christmas," and playing the Christmas carol "O Holy Night" on his violin.

Radio broadcasts, including live opera music and election results, quickly became popular. The first broadcasts were difficult to hear but, as equipment improved, sound became clearer. In 1920, the first **commercial** radio station, KDKA, was established in Pittsburgh, Pennsylvania. By 1935, two out of three American households owned a radio. Radio stations across the United States offered a rich variety of programs, such as children's shows, comedy series, and dramas.

(left) An illustrator from the 1890s imagines a time when people will be able to enjoy a live concert from home, with the help of receivers and a screen.

Images by Wire

Many inventions in the 1800s allowed people to transmit images from one place to another. Several of these inventions led to the development of the television.

The Facsimile Machine

In 1843, Scottish inventor Alexander Bain proposed an idea that became the basis for the facsimile, or fax, machine, a device that sends and receives images. In the 1860s, the Italian inventor Giovanni Caselli developed the first widely used fax machine, which he called the pantelegraph. The pantelegraph converted handwriting and drawings into electrical signals, which were sent over wires. A machine at the other end received the signals and traced the original message on paper.

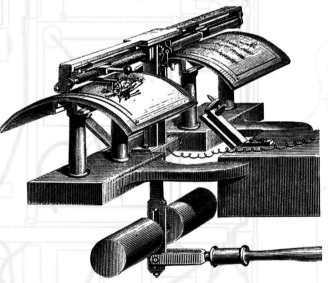

(above) "Pantelegraph" combines the words "pantograph," a tool that copies drawings, and "telegraph."

(top) No one is sure if George Carey ever built his selenium camera, shown here in one of his sketches.

The Selenium Camera

In the 1870s, an American named George Carey drew plans for a camera that sent images over wires. Carey's plan was to divide an image up into parts. Each part would be transmitted, or sent, separately to a receiver, which was a panel, or grouping, of light bulbs. Inside Carey's camera was a metal plate filled with tiny pieces of selenium, a chemical that carries electricity when light shines on it. Each piece of selenium was connected by a wire to one light bulb in the panel. When an object was photographed, the light that reflected off the object would enter the camera through a **lens**. The selenium would convert the light into electrical signals that would be sent to the light bulbs. A picture would be seen on the receiver when the light bulbs lit up in a pattern that re-created the image.

The Nipkow Disk

In the 1880s, German inventor Paul Nipkow drew plans for a disk, known as the Nipkow disk, that was used in many of the first television systems. The disk was pierced with holes in a spiral pattern. A live, moving scene could be **scanned** with one turn of the disc.

According to Nipkow's plans, light bouncing from a moving scene would pass through the disk's holes and strike selenium. This would create an electrical signal that would be transmitted over a wire. When the signal reached a light bulb at the other end of the wire, the bulb would light up. The light from the bulb would pass through a second spinning disk to re-create the image on a screen. Each time the disk made a full turn, it would transmit a new image. When sent quickly one after the other, the images would appear to move.

How We See Images

Images produced by Nipkow's disk appeared to move for the same reason that cartoons in a flipbook do. In a flipbook, almost exactly the same scene is drawn on each page, but the drawings are actually steps in a sequence. When the pages of the book are flipped, and the human eye sees more than ten images per second, the drawings appear as one moving scene. The faster the images are displayed, the smoother the movement appears.

Nipkow never built a working model of his invention. His disk was the basis for televisions built 40 years later, such as those by Scottish inventor John Logie Baird.

Mechanical Televisions

I n the 1920s, two inventors built improved, working versions of Nipkow's invention to create the first television systems. Their televisions became known as mechanical televisions because they relied on moving parts.

J. L. Baird and his Mechanical Television

John Logie Baird received a **patent** for his mechanical television in 1924. The disk in Baird's television camera, or transmitter, used pieces of selenium that were more **sensitive** to light than those in Nipkow's model, making the images clearer.

The first images that Baird transmitted using his mechanical television were of objects, such as a cross and a paper mask, that he moved in front of the camera. The images appeared on a screen as moving "shadowgraphs." Shadowgraphs are silhouettes, or outlines, that show no detail.

John Logie Baird's first television system sent images as electrical signals over telephone wires. Later, Baird developed a way to send images by radio waves.

Demonstrating his Invention

In 1925, Baird demonstrated his work for amazed spectators at Selfridges, a large department store in London, England. After the demonstration, he worked to improve his invention. In 1926, in a workshop in his attic, Baird transmitted a detailed, moving image of a human face for a group of visiting scientists.

Televisors

Baird's first television receivers, or sets, called "Televisors," were sold in Britain in 1928. There were three different models. The least expensive model had to be connected to a radio to receive sound, while the other two models had built-in speakers. The public was interested in the new television sets, but the picture was extremely fuzzy, and there was almost no programming to watch except for the experimental broadcasts that Baird produced himself.

Baird worked to improve his system so that it could transmit more than just silhouettes, such as this image of a human face.

All three Televisor models had rectangular screens measuring two square inches (13 square centimeters). A magnifying glass in front of each screen, shown on the right side of this television cabinet, enlarged the image.

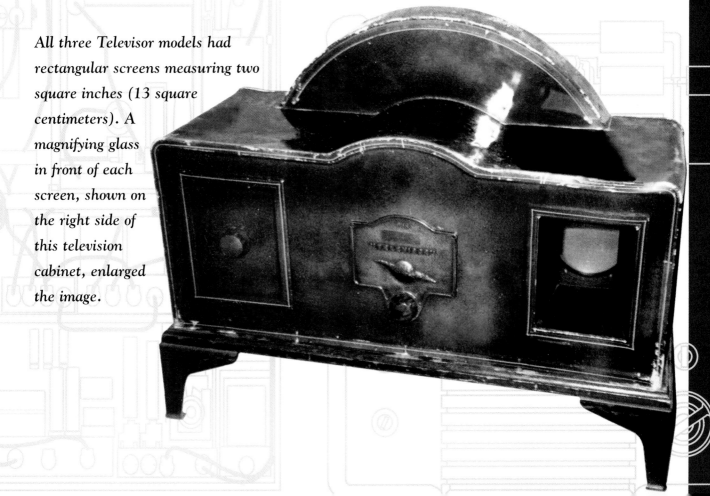

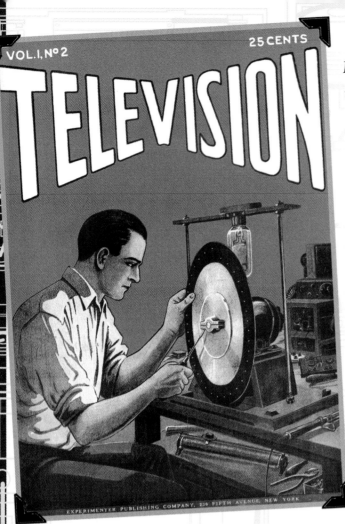

VOL. I, Nº 2

25 CENTS

TELEVISION

EXPERIMENTER PUBLISHING COMPANY, 230 FIFTH AVENUE, NEW YORK

Early television enthusiasts bought magazines that described advances in television technology. On this magazine cover from 1928, a man repairs a Nipkow disk.

C. F. Jenkins and Radiovision

While Baird was working in Britain, Charles Francis Jenkins patented his own mechanical television system, called radiovision, in the United States. Instead of using a Nipkow disk, radiovision used a drum pierced with holes to scan images. Jenkins' receivers consisted of small viewing screens that displayed images that were two square inches (13 square centimeters). Separate radios allowed sound to accompany the pictures. Jenkins also sold cheap television kits so that people who already owned radios could turn them into radiovision receivers.

Baird and the BBC

In 1929, Baird began to broadcast programs from his own studio over the radio **transmitter** owned by the British Broadcasting Corporation (BBC), the main radio broadcaster in the **United Kingdom**. Baird's programs, which included variety shows and plays, aired before the BBC's morning radio programs and after its late evening radio programs.

At first, the sound and image signals of Baird's programs could not be sent over the air at the same time, so the broadcasts consisted of two minutes of sound followed by two minutes of images. In 1930, pictures and sound were transmitted at the same time and, by 1932, the BBC was broadcasting its own programming. Interest in television increased so much that, by 1939, about 20,000 Baird Televisors had been sold in Britain.

Jenkins, shown here, later developed a mechanical television that had a screen on top to view the picture, and a speaker on the bottom for the sound.

Watching Radiovision

At Jenkins' first official demonstration of his system in 1925, he transmitted a ten-minute film showing a moving toy windmill. Three years later, Jenkins was transmitting "radiomovies" from his own television station in Washington, D.C. The radiomovies were shown for a few hours, six nights per week, across the eastern United States. The quality of the images was very poor, and viewers had to constantly adjust knobs on their sets to make the picture clearer. In spite of the poor quality, as many as 20,000 people regularly tuned in.

Jenkins' radiomovies featured silhouette images of his employees and local children dancing, skipping rope, or bouncing balls.

In an effort to boost sales, this 1932 advertisement for Jenkins' television system describes the equipment as "attractive," "simple to operate," and "quiet."

Electronic Televisions

I n the 1920s, around the same time that mechanical televisions were being developed, Philo T. Farnsworth and Vladimir Zworykin were building electronic televisions. Electronic televisions have no moving parts, and they transmit pictures that are much sharper and steadier than those of mechanical televisions.

The Cathode-Ray Tube

Electronic TVs use cathode-ray tubes, or CRTs, to capture images at the transmitting end and re-create them at the receiving end. The CRT was developed by German scientist Karl Ferdinand Braun in 1897. When a wire, called a cathode, is heated inside the tube, it sends a cathode ray, or a stream of electrically charged particles called electrons, toward the tube's screen. Devices called anodes focus and accelerate the ray. The screen is coated with phosphor, a material that glows when hit by a cathode ray. The parts of the screen that do not get hit by the ray remain dark.

Zworykin's Electronic Television

Vladimir Zworykin, a Russian-born inventor working in the United States, developed an electronic television system based on the cathode-ray tube. The iconoscope, Zworykin's television camera tube, created an image from a live scene, scanned the image, and turned it into an electrical signal. The electrical signal traveled as radio waves to Zworykin's television set.

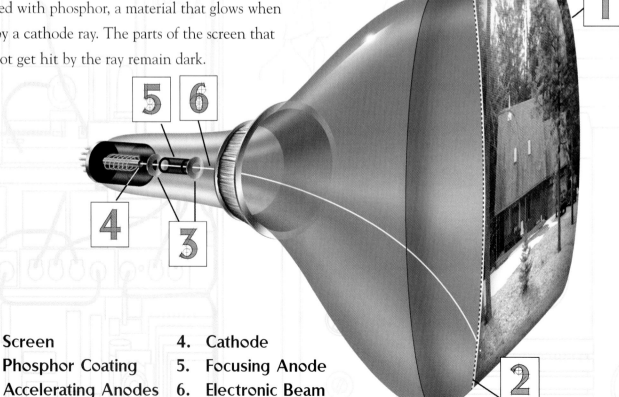

1. Screen
2. Phosphor Coating
3. Accelerating Anodes
4. Cathode
5. Focusing Anode
6. Electronic Beam

Vladimir Zworykin received a patent for his iconoscope, shown here, in 1938. Camera tubes such as the iconoscope formed the basis for television cameras for 40 years.

The Kinescope

When Zworykin's television set received the signal, a cathode ray inside the kinescope, or picture tube, swept across the tube's phosphor-coated screen from left to right. This action created tiny glowing points of light, or pixels, wherever the ray struck. Thousands of pixels made up the image that appeared on the screen. Eventually, Zworykin's system was able to send 30 images every second. This created the impression of a moving scene.

Philo T. Farnsworth, shown here with his wife, designed a workable television system while still in high school.

Philo T. Farnsworth

In 1926, at the age of 20, Philo T. Farnsworth set up a laboratory where he conducted experiments in the hopes of inventing a working electronic television system. During the next few years, he was able to transmit simple images: a straight line, then a triangle, then a dollar sign.

Like Zworykin's system, Farnsworth's camera used a cathode-ray tube, which he called an image dissector, to scan images. In his television set, another cathode-ray tube, which he called an image oscillite, displayed the images. Farnsworth applied for a patent for his system in 1927, and the patent was granted in 1930.

Selling to the World

Beginning in the mid-1930s, broadcasters in England and Germany were using the electronic television system rather than the mechanical system. By 1939, electronic TVs were the popular choice in many areas of Europe and were finally sold in the United States.

This postcard shows The Hall of Special Events at the 1939 World's Fair, held in Flushing Meadows, New York.

A Fair Invention

In the United States, a disagreement over patents between the Radio Corporation of America (RCA), where Zworykin began working in the 1930s, and Philo T. Farnsworth delayed the launch of electronic television until 1939. The launch took place at the New York World's Fair, where new inventions were introduced to the public. Other manufacturers demonstrated their television sets at the fair, as well. The New York World's Fair ran for 18 months and drew 45 million visitors, who enjoyed a welcome break from the recent **Great Depression** and fears about an upcoming world war.

Seeing the Big Picture

Television demonstrations at the fair amazed audiences, many of whom were seeing television for the first time. Visitors waved at television cameras outside the fair buildings, while others saw the scenes broadcast on television sets inside. Models of living rooms with televisions were displayed, so visitors could see how televisions could be part of their homes.

(left) The National Broadcasting Corporation (NBC), the broadcasting company owned by RCA, began regular broadcasts on April 30, 1939, at the World's Fair. Viewers watched as President Franklin D. Roosevelt opened the fair with a speech.

A Luxury Item

In 1939, four different models of RCA television sets were available to consumers, ranging in price from $200 to $600. These sets were too expensive for most Americans, who earned only about $35 per week. The most affordable set was a small television that could be placed on a table, but it only displayed images. To receive sound, the television had to be connected with a wire to a radio. The more expensive models incorporated radios into their design, but the sets were large and bulky.

Since televisions were expensive, early advertisements were aimed at the wealthy. These ads presented televisions as desirable luxury items, and showed people watching television in fancy evening wear.

Today's most welcome gift....

GOWNS BY BERGDORF-GOODMAN

You will enjoy television at its finest on the big, brilliant, *direct-view* screen of a Du Mont— whether it is a simple table-top receiver, or one of the magnificent luxury models.

Illustrated: The Du Mont Savoy: 72 sq. in. direct-view screen; AM and FM radio; automatic record player. $795 plus installation.

DUMONT FIRST WITH THE FINEST IN TELEVISION

Television Takes Off

At first, few people bought televisions because few programs were available. The television industry also suffered during World War II, because television factories stopped producing televisions to make supplies for the war.

The Effect of the War

Before the war began, television viewers watched cartoons, musical performances, live sporting events, and cooking demonstrations. Almost all broadcasting stopped during World War II. When Britain entered the war, the BBC's broadcasting came to a halt in the middle of a Mickey Mouse cartoon. When the war ended, the BBC began broadcasting again at the exact point in the cartoon where it had stopped six years before.

When televisions were first introduced, appliance stores put them in their front windows, causing crowds to gather.

Greater Interest

After the war, people had more money to spend and more time to relax in front of television sets. New television stations were established, and the number and types of programs increased. Children's shows, westerns, comedies, and variety programs became popular, and special events were televised. In the United States, the 1947 World Series of baseball attracted a huge audience. People who did not have televisions in their homes went to local diners and bars to watch the games.

Television Production Increases

As people became more interested in watching television, manufacturers began producing more TV sets, with more affordable prices. Between 1946 and 1953, the number of television sets in the United States jumped from 20,000 to more than 20 million. Television had started to take the place of radio and movies as a main source of news and entertainment.

The Howdy Doody Show, *featuring marionettes and live actors, was a popular children's show in the 1950s.*

The Program Guide

In the 1940s, broadcasters sent out postcards to television set owners, listing the week's program offerings. Later, they placed small advertisements in local newspapers. As the number of television networks and the number of shows on the air increased, three small weekly magazines in different parts of the United States began printing the network listings. In 1953, they joined together to create the national magazine *TV Guide*.

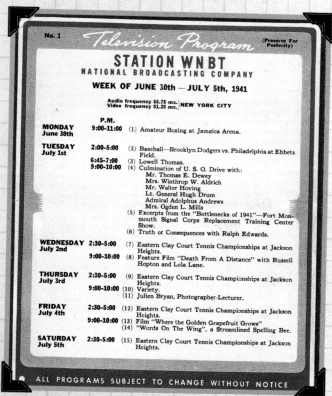

In the early years, television stations broadcast for only a few hours each day, as seen in this program guide from 1941.

A Burst of Color

O nce televisions were launched, manufacturers and broadcasters worked together to make the television-viewing experience more exciting. After more than a decade of experimentation, they introduced color televisions to the public.

The First Color Images

The first televisions showed only black-and-white images. In 1928, John Logie Baird transmitted the first color images on his mechanical television, including one of a man sticking out his tongue. Another mechanical color television system was invented in the 1940s, but it was not practical. The black-and-white sets that most people had at the time could not display pictures from color transmissions, and showed only static.

Ads for color televisions promised people a more lifelike viewing experience.

Color Television

In 1954, RCA launched an electronic color system that worked with both black-and-white and color television sets. The transmission, or electrical signal, sent by this new system carried color programming but was also able to re-create clear images on black-and-white televisions. Few people bought RCA's color televisions because they were expensive, and most programming was still in black and white. By 1960, many manufacturers had stopped producing color televisions because of poor sales.

In 1954, RCA's first color television sold for a suggested retail price of $1,000 — about the same price as a new car at that time.

Changing to Color

The next year, a popular black-and-white show that combined cartoon and live-action entertainment began broadcasting in color. The family show, renamed *Walt Disney's Wonderful World of Color*, helped publicize color television, and many people bought color sets as a result. Networks began to produce more color programming and, by the end of the 1960s, most television shows were in color.

Bonanza, *a western filmed in color, first aired on September 12, 1959. The show was made by NBC as a way of improving sales of color televisions made by NBC's owner, RCA.*

Seeing Color

In black-and-white televisions, the phosphor coating on the back of the screen glows white where it is struck by the cathode ray, and appears black where the beam does not strike. In color televisions, each pixel is made up of three phosphor dots that glow red, green, or blue.

Color televisions also have three cathode rays — one for each color. To make the color blue, the blue ray strikes the phosphor that glows blue. A similar process results in the colors red and green. Different combinations of glowing red, green, and blue dots produce all other colors. Purple, for example, is a combination of red and blue glowing dots, which a person's eyes blend together.

The Jetsons, *a cartoon series set in the future, debuted in color in 1962.*

Getting a Signal

Television signals travel in different ways and in different forms. Analog signals consist of waves of electricity that weaken as they cross distances, resulting in a loss of picture quality. Digital signals are electronic signals that do not change during transmission, so images and sound are always crisp.

"Rabbit Ears"

Until the late 1940s, television sets used antennas to capture radio wave signals sent over the air. Some antennas, known as "rabbit ears," sat on top of television sets, while other antennas were placed on roofs to capture signals from farther away. Even with antennas, **reception** was poor outside of cities, where signals originated. Tall buildings, hills and mountains, storms, and passing airplanes interfered with the signals.

People still use antennas today, but these usually only catch signals from local television stations.

1924	1925	1930	1939	1948	1954
John Logie Baird receives a patent for his mechanical television.	Charles Francis Jenkins gives the first official demonstration of his mechanical television system, called radiovision.	Philo T. Farnsworth receives a patent for his electronic television system.	The Radio Corporation of America (RCA) launches Vladimir Zworykin's electronic television at the World's Fair.	Cable television is first used to bring programs to remote areas.	RCA launches its electronic color televisions.

Cable Television

In 1948, people in three small towns in Oregon, Pennsylvania, and Arkansas all found a way to improve the television reception in their communities, which were surrounded by hills and mountains. They placed large antennas on tops of peaks and hilltops to catch the television signals, and ran cables from the antennas to people's television sets. The signals traveled through the cables to produce clearer pictures. As time went on, cable service expanded to other areas.

Communication satellites transmit television signals in a straight path to satellite dishes on Earth, or pass them to other space satellites that serve distant parts of the world.

In 1970, cable companies began using fiber-optic cable, which is made of glass or plastic strands. Compared to traditional cable, fiber-optic cable provides better-quality images and more channels to choose from.

Satellite Television

Since 1973, communication satellites positioned high in space have transmitted very clear television signals back to Earth. Satellites allow people to receive programs from all around the world almost instantly. The signals are captured by special antennas called satellite dishes, which many people buy and place outside their homes.

1973	1977	1996	1998	1999	2000
Satellites are first regularly used in television broadcasting.	The VHS videocassette format is launched in Japan and the U.S.	Toshiba and Matsushita introduce the digital videodisk (DVD) player in Japan.	The first high-definition television sets are sold in North America.	Digital video recorders (DVRs) are sold.	Internet broadcasting is introduced in the United Kingdom.

Inside a Television

When a television camera captures moving pictures, the light from the scene is changed into electrical signals. Radio waves carry the picture signal, as well as the sound signal, over the air to the television set. This diagram shows how a color cathode-ray tube television works.

1. Power source: Televisions plug into standard wall sockets. Some smaller televisions also run on battery power.

2. Tuner: The tuner receives the sound and picture signals coming into the television, and passes them to amplifiers.

3. Amplifiers: First invented in 1906, amplifiers strengthen the electrical signals that tuners receive, then send them to CRTs and speakers.

4. Electron gun: The electron gun, which includes the cathode and anodes, creates the cathode rays.

Screen

Cathode rays

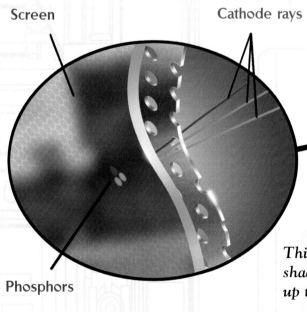

Phosphors

This up-close view of the television screen and shadow mask shows the cathode rays lighting up the three different colors of phosphor dots.

5. Steering coils: Two sets of steering coils, carrying electric currents, wind around the cathode-ray tube. The electric current creates a **magnetic field** that moves the cathode rays left to right, in lines, or rows, across the screen. When the rays reach the bottom right of the screen, they pass back up to the top left and start over. In most North American CRT televisions, the cathode rays scan 525 lines.

6. Shadow mask: The shadow mask is a thin screen with hundreds of thousands of tiny holes. The holes guide the cathode rays so that they strike the phosphor dots precisely.

7. Speakers: Most television sets have built-in speakers, but many people prefer to connect their sets to separate sound systems, which can provide better sound quality.

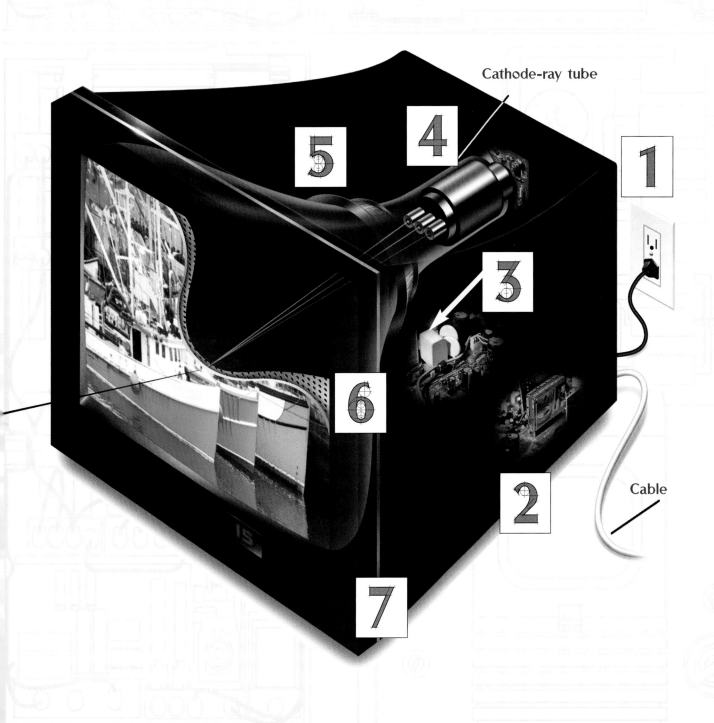

Cathode-ray tube

Cable

New and Improved

T he mid- to late 1900s saw many changes in television technology. Televisions were produced in many different sizes, sound and picture quality improved, and televisions without CRTs were introduced. Inventions that allowed viewers to watch programs at their convenience also became common.

Remote Controls

In 1950, the Zenith Radio Corporation introduced the world's first television remote control, called Lazy Bones. Connected to a television by a cable, it allowed people to change channels and adjust the volume without getting out of their chairs. Five years later, Zenith released the first wireless remote control, the Flash-Matic, which worked by aiming a beam of light at sensors on a television set. Today's television remote controls send signals as **infrared** rays of light.

Going Flat

In the past, CRT screens were slightly rounded. Flat screens, introduced in 1998, have less **glare** than rounded screens, and the entire picture is very clear. Images on rounded screens are less sharp and more distorted, or pulled out of shape, around the edges.

Plasma and **liquid crystal display (LCD)** TV screens first appeared in the late 1990s and early 2000s, and have begun to replace CRT screens. These flat-panel screens are thin enough to be mounted on walls or hung from ceilings.

LCD technology, such as that used on this display screen, requires less power than CRT technology.

(above) This early remote control from England allowed viewers to choose from three channels, indicated by the buttons at the top.

Television for All

Television has been adapted so that people with hearing and vision loss can enjoy programming. In closed-captioning, a service introduced in 1980, the script of a television show, as well as captions for sounds such as "stairs creaking" or "owl hooting," appear on the screen. Described video is a service that "speaks" to viewers, telling them what happens when the actors are not talking. This ensures that people with vision loss do not miss parts of the show.

Jumbo TV screens are often set up in sports arenas and concert halls. This screen is in Times Square in New York City. It shows news reports, commercials, and other TV programs.

High-Definition Television

The first digital high-definition television sets were sold in North America in 1998. High-definition signals deliver images that are broken up into many more pieces than regular television signals, and high-definition television sets read the signals. The result is a much sharper, more finely detailed image than that of cathode-ray tube televisions, with as many as 1,080 lines making up the picture, and much crisper sound.

Watching Television Anytime

For many decades, viewers either watched a show as it aired or missed it entirely. Videocassette recorders (VCRs), introduced in the late 1970s, allowed people to record programs on videocassette tapes, then watch them later on their VCRs. Today, digital video recorders (DVRs) save shows in digital format on digital videodisks (DVDs) or on the DVRs' **hard drives**. Viewers can watch shows recorded on hard drives as they are being broadcast, pausing the shows if necessary, or they can watch the shows later.

Watching Television

Television has had an enormous influence on people's lives. Audiences in every country, from every age group and level of income, watch television each day, and hundreds of thousands of people work in industries related to television.

(above) Many people in the television industry work behind the scenes as technicians, writers, directors, and camera operators.

Television Programs

In the early days of television, programs were broadcast for only a few hours each day, and there were few channels to choose from. Today, a wide range of channels broadcast many different types of programs, day and night. Viewers can watch sitcoms, dramas, reality programs, news programs, talk shows, sports events, cooking shows, and much more. People who are interested in a particular topic can watch specialty channels, which devote their entire schedules to one type of program, such as music, cartoons, or game shows.

For many people, watching television is more than just a way to relax after a busy day. Television programs can educate and inspire people. Many programs tackle difficult real-life topics, which can help people understand these issues better.

In 1969, more than 600 million people around the world watched on television as astronauts walked on the Moon for the first time.

Viewer Control

Many people are concerned about what children see on television, especially the amount of violence. In 1998, Canadian inventor Tim Collings patented the V-chip. "V" stands for "viewer control." With this invention, adults can block shows that they consider unsuitable from their television sets. A dark screen appears when someone tries to watch a show that has been "blocked."

Many toddlers and young children spend more time watching television than playing, participating in sports, reading, and doing other activities that have been linked to good health and school performance.

The Nielsen Household

Broadcasters conduct surveys to find out what people watch. They use this information to plan which programs to air so they attract the largest audiences.

Since the 1950s, the Nielsen's People Meter has gathered information about Americans' television viewing habits from tens of thousands of households. Boxes placed on top of televisions, VCRs, and DVD players note every show viewed or recorded. All members of the household press their own buttons on the boxes to record their viewing choices. Other Nielsen households record, in week-long diaries, what television programs they watch, and when.

More than a TV

S ince the days of the earliest experimental broadcasts, many inventors who developed television had more than just a source of entertainment in mind. Today, television is used in many different ways, from ordering goods to teaching doctors new ways to perform surgery.

Not Just Television Programs

At home, people do more with their televisions than ever before. Viewers connect their televisions to DVD players or VCRs, as well as **surround-sound systems**, and watch movies in "home theaters." They participate in interactive television, a service that gets viewers more involved with the programs they watch. Viewers can choose the camera angle for a sports game, play along with a game show, and even order pizza, all with the help of a remote control and a special box that sits on top of the television.

People in various jobs use televisions in their training. Flight simulators allow pilots to practice operating airplanes in different conditions.

Closed-Circuit Television

In closed-circuit television, cameras and television sets are joined together in a closed network. There is no way for television sets outside the network to receive the television signal.

Closed-circuit television has many uses, including observing patients who are receiving treatments in hospitals and monitoring traffic for traffic reports. In some towns and cities, closed-circuit televisions record activity in banks and stores. This discourages people from committing crimes, since the recordings can identify them as criminals.

Children and adults play games using video game consoles that are connected to televisions.

Videoconferencing

Videoconferencing is a system that allows people in different locations to see each other as they talk to one another. At first, videoconferences combined closed-circuit television and telephone technology. To hold a videoconference today, most people use computers with **Internet** access and special **software**. They also need Web cams, which are small cameras that deliver images over the Internet, and microphones and speakers, which are sometimes built into the cameras or computers. People can also hold videoconferences using videophones, which are telephones with built-in screens and cameras.

Images from TV monitors in operating rooms can be transmitted to television sets in other locations, so that medical students and colleagues can learn new surgical techniques.

Computers have CRT, plasma, or LCD screens, just like televisions.

Medical Uses

High-definition video cameras and screens are lifesaving tools in hospital operating rooms. During surgeries, doctors often use laparoscopes, or narrow tube-shaped video cameras, which are inserted into patients' bodies through small incisions, or cuts. The images from the cameras appear on television screens that surgeons watch to see what is happening inside the bodies.

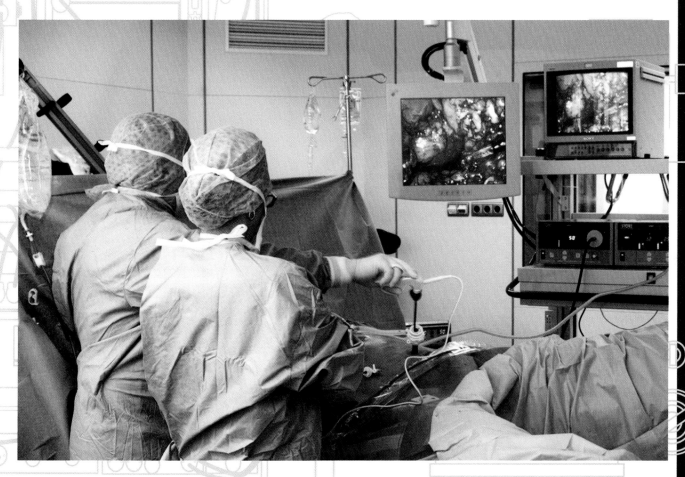

Television Tomorrow

M ore and more, televisions are being combined with other technologies, so single devices can accomplish many tasks. For example, cellular, or cell, phones are now available with built-in television screens. These phones make it more convenient for viewers to watch television anytime and anywhere.

Internet Broadcasting

Watching television programs, broadcast from anywhere in the world, on a computer screen will soon become more common. Internet broadcasting gives viewers more choice of what to watch, and it allows people who create television programs to broadcast their shows without the help of traditional television stations. Some television "channels" have been created especially for the Internet, and cannot be viewed on television sets. Many traditional television stations also broadcast their regular programs on the Internet, or broadcast special video clips, such as award-show performances and talk-show interviews, which viewers pay to watch.

(above) Owners of television phones can watch live television programs, download short versions of popular programs from the Internet, or watch full television episodes and feature films that are stored on removable memory cards.

Coming up Next

Television viewers will soon be able to turn their televisions on and off and change channels with voice-controlled remote controls. The remote controls will recognize viewers' voices and carry out their requests.

Parents who worry that their children spend too much time watching television and not enough time doing physical activities may soon be able to turn their children's television time into rewards for exercise. "Smart shoes" count their wearers' footsteps, and send this information to televisions. The televisions stay on for one minute for every 100 steps taken.

3-D Television

Several three-dimensional (3-D) video display systems are being developed today, with a few now available for sale. Some monitors require viewers to wear 3-D goggles, while others have special lighting and **filters** behind the screens to create 3-D effects without goggles. Special boxes that sit on top of televisions turn ordinary two-dimensional broadcasts into three-dimensional ones when viewed on televisions that are "3-D ready." Cell phones that display 3-D television are being developed as well.

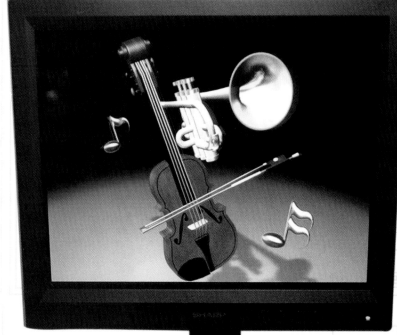

(above right) This flat-panel television set uses special software to add depth to a DVD recording, creating a three-dimensional image.

Holographic Television

A system of holographic television, which re-creates miniature, 3-D moving scenes in special deep television sets, is being developed by a team of American scientists. The images will be captured by several video cameras, each of which will record the scene from a different angle. At the receiving end, beams of laser light, bouncing off close to one million mirrored panels, will display the images.

(left) While a 3-D television has images that appear to pop out of the screen, holographic televisions, such as the one shown here, appear to suspend images in mid-air.

Glossary

antenna A device used to send and receive television or radio signals

commercial Established to make money and, as in the case of radio and TV stations, often funded by advertisers

download To receive a file sent over a computer network

filter A device that allows only certain things, such as certain types of light, to pass through it

glare A strong, bright light that makes it difficult to see

Great Depression A period of mass unemployment and poverty in the 1930s

hard drive A piece of computer equipment that stores information and reads data from disks, CDs, or DVDs

infrared Relating to a particular type of invisible light

Internet A network of more than 100 million computers that communicate and share information with one another

lens A curved piece of glass or plastic that focuses the light rays entering a camera

liquid crystal display (LCD) A display on an electronic device consisting of liquid crystal. The display darkens in areas where an electric current passes through the liquid crystal, and an image is created by the combination of light and dark areas

magnetic field The area around a magnet or an electric current where magnetic forces are found

memory card A removable device that stores data for digital cameras, laptop computers, cellular phones, and other electronic equipment

patent A legal document that prevents people from using inventors' ideas for a certain period of time without giving them proper recognition and payment

plasma A type of display that produces an image by releasing a gas, causing phosphors to give off colored light

receiver A device that receives electrical signals and converts them into sound or pictures

reception The quality of the signal received by a television or radio

satellite An object that circles Earth or another planet, sometimes transmitting communication signals

scan To sweep a beam of light or electrons over a scene in order to reproduce an image

sensitive To react, or respond, quickly

software A computer program or application

surround-sound system A sound system designed to make listeners feel as though they are surrounded by sound

transmitter A device used to broadcast radio or television signals

United Kingdom A country off the coast of northwestern Europe consisting of England, Scotland, Wales, and Northern Ireland

variety show A show made up of comedy skits, songs, dances, and other short performances

World War II An international war fought mostly in Europe and Asia from 1939 to 1945

Index

1 2 3 4 5 6 7 8 9 0 Printed in the U.S.A. 5 4 3 2 1 0 9 8 7 6